Original title:
The Succulent Soul

Copyright © 2025 Creative Arts Management OÜ
All rights reserved.

Author: Alec Donovan
ISBN HARDBACK: 978-1-80581-795-6
ISBN PAPERBACK: 978-1-80581-322-4
ISBN EBOOK: 978-1-80581-795-6

Oasis of Loving Shadows

In a garden where giggles bloom,
Cacti wear sombreros, chasing gloom.
Silly lizards in a dance parade,
Stealing sunbeams, never afraid.

Puns grow ripe like juicy fruit,
Hummingbirds wear tiny boots.
With every chuckle, we grow wide,
In this playful patch where we abide.

Flourish in the Heart's Garden

Petals sprout from jokes we tell,
Sunshine winks, all is well.
Daisies laugh with mocking grace,
While mushrooms dance, and squirrels race.

Giggly weeds in every nook,
A poetic plot, well worth a look.
Laughter spills from every vine,
In this lively space, we intertwine.

Harvesting Joy in Abundance

Baskets filled with puns and glee,
Cucumbers giggle with such esprit.
Tomatoes blush at playful jokes,
While cornfields sway with cheerful folks.

Every fruit's a joke in disguise,
Ripe for laughter, oh what a prize!
Come join the feast, don't be late,
In this harvest, we celebrate.

The Unfolding Patchwork of Existence

Quirky quilts stitched with care,
Moments of joy thread everywhere.
Each patch a tale of silly flair,
Colorful laughter fills the air.

Snug in sunshine, wrapped in cheer,
Witty whispers, lend your ear.
In every fold, a story spun,
Life's a laugh, let's have some fun!

Harvesting Hope from Thorns

In gardens lush, we find our jest,
Where prickles hide a leafy fest.
With laughter loud, we prune the fear,
And find the blooms in spite of sneers.

A cactus dance, it sways and shakes,
Its pointy hugs can give us aches.
But every thorn that pokes and prods,
Can still unveil a smile from gods.

The Art of Growing through Adversity

In rocky soil, we plant our seeds,
With grit and grime, we tend our needs.
A little rain, a lot of sun,
We'll laugh and grow, it's all in fun.

The weeds may come, they try to snatch,
We pull them out, a comical match.
In gardens wild, we find our way,
With humor bright, we seize the day.

Radiance in the Desert Wind

The desert breeze, it tickles pink,
A cactus grin, it makes us think.
Amidst the dunes, we find our flair,
With sun-kissed laughter filling the air.

The stones may roll, and tumble down,
But we'll don smiles, no room for frowns.
With every gust, we sway and laugh,
In sandy paths, we find our craft.

Shadows that Nurture

Beneath the shade of leafy dreams,
We share our hopes with sprightly schemes.
In shadowed corners, laughter blooms,
A cheeky dance amongst the glooms.

With muffled giggles, roots entwine,
To nurture growth, oh, isn't it fine?
In every shade, we sip the sun,
With wit and whim, the soul we've won.

Ebb and Flow of Tenderness

Softly does the laughter ring,
As joy and silliness take wing.
Frogs in bow ties, dancing so bright,
Puddle splashes of pure delight.

Tickle the petals, send them a tease,
Watch them giggle in the warm breeze.
A hug from a leaf, a wink from a bud,
Growing together in this sweet mud.

Garden of Quenching Dreams

Twirling daisies in a hat,
Dreams watering can, imagine that!
Sunflowers juggling, what a sight,
In the garden, laughter takes flight.

Dandelion wishes on a trampoline,
Bouncing high, not so serene.
A worm wearing specs reads the news,
While bees perform in striped shoes.

Whispers of Resilience

Bamboo giggles, bending away,
Laughing storms, come what may.
Wiggly roots in belly laughs,
Digging deep for the choicest gaffs.

A cactus wearing a smile so bright,
Hugging itself, what a funny sight!
Through prickles and woes, it doesn't pout,
It's the quirky charm that life's about.

Nectar in a Gilded Dawn

Morning nectar with a splash,
Honeybees buzzing, making a dash.
Sunrise giggles, soft hues abound,
With every bloom, joy is found.

Breakfast of laughter served on a plate,
Mimosa petals, isn't that great?
Droplets of sunshine, all aglow,
With every drop, see the spirits grow.

Embers at Dusk

In the twilight glow, the cacti dance,
Their spines like disco balls, taking a chance.
A tumbleweed rolls past with a wheezy laugh,
While the moon joins in for a crazy photograph.

Chasing shadows, a lizard takes flight,
Performing acrobatics in the fading light.
He trips on his tail, oh what a blunder,
As the stars erupt, like bursts of thunder.

The Heart's Hidden Garden

In a patch of greens where oddballs bloom,
A donut-shaped plant dreams of the moon.
With a wink and a wiggle, it makes quite a fuss,
Yelling, "I'm sweet!" while the others just cuss.

A pear in a pickle, a joker too bold,
Tells jokes to the lettuce, who's starting to mold.
"Lettuce turnip the beet!" he chimes with a grin,
While the carrots just groan, rolling their eyes in spin.

Cultivating Quiet Fortitude

A succulent sits, with a smile on its face,
Sipping from dew in its cozy little space.
With roots deep in laughter, it sways to the beat,
That life gives you lemons, it's the best kind of treat.

Bouncing in rhythm, this plant loves to play,
Thinking of puns as it sways all day.
It whispers to weeds, "Don't worry, my friends,
Let's embrace our quirks; this fun never ends!"

Serenity in Spiky Embrace

In a forest of misfits, where chaos is king,
Spiky friends hold hands, a curious thing.
"Hey there!" says a thistle, with flair and some pride,
"Let's form a band!" then rolls with the tide.

They strum on their needles, a prickly delight,
And sing of the sunshine that never feels bright.
"Cactus, you're sharp!" cries a flower in glee,
"But that's why I adore your spiky esprit!"

Breath of the Unfurling Heart

In a garden of giggles, blooms take flight,
They wiggle and wiggle, what a funny sight!
With petals like sneakers, they dance on one foot,
Swirling in laughter, oh, how cute!

They whisper sweet secrets, all afternoon,
Making jokes with dandelions, a fellow buffoon.
Even the daisies can't help but chuckle,
When the breeze plays tag, oh what a shuffle!

Petals of Perseverance

These petals are fighters, not afraid to fall,
With worms as their audience, they give it their all.
They stretch toward the sky with silly poses,
While bees crack up over the ridiculous roses.

When the rain starts to pour, they wear little hats,
And dance in puddles, like giggling spats.
'We won't let the wetness ruin our fun!'
They shout as they splash, 'Come everyone!'

Blooming Under Moonlight

Under the moon, the garden throws a bash,
With petals like confetti and lights all agash.
The night is a backdrop for this bright affair,
Where flowers do flips without a single care.

Starlit laughter fills the fragrant scene,
As tulips do the tango, the oddest routine.
With crickets as the band playing tunes so fun,
The blossoms know how to have a great run!

Lush Echoes of Serenity

In this land of green, mischief takes root,
As leaves start to chuckle, giving a hoot.
The vines share a jest, climbing higher with glee,
Swapping hilarious tales with the tallest of trees.

Each whisper of wind carries jokes to the sky,
As the petals burst out, 'Oh my, oh my!'
They tickle the senses, with humor so spry,
In this verdant expanse, let laughter fly high!

The Veil of Grit and Bloom

In a garden where laughter grows,
Twirling cacti wear silly clothes.
Petals giggle in the sun,
As bees buzz by just for fun.

Leaves dance lightly in the breeze,
Whispering secrets like old bees.
Thorns chuckle at their plight,
Spreading joy both day and night.

So come and sip the dew of cheer,
In this patch where friends draw near.
Let your worries take a snooze,
With each bloom, there's joy to choose.

When the laughter bursts like blooms,
Blame it on the silly grooms.
With wiggle-worms and giggle-guys,
Life's a feast under sunny skies.

Stories Written in the Sand

Footprints waltz on grains so fine,
Teaching crabs to toe the line.
Seagulls squawk their latest news,
As shells wear glittery party shoes.

Each wave whispers a silly tale,
Of lost flip-flops, boats, and sail.
Sandcastles crumble with a smile,
Rising back up, just to defile.

The tide brings secrets; oh what glee,
What mischief hides in the salty spree?
Laughter echoed in the foam,
Each grain of sand feels like home.

So let's scribble our dreams anew,
With jellyfish ink in vivid hue.
Stories dance before they fade,
In every nook, a memory made.

Panoramas of Life and Quietude

A garden sprawls under the sun,
Worms wear shades, just having fun.
Butterflies don't give a care,
While ants perform a funny dare.

In this world of silly sights,
Plants don capes and fly like kites.
Sunflowers laugh as they reach tall,
Every whisper turns into a brawl.

Grains of pollen swirl around,
As flower frogs hop and astound.
Chasing rainbows, they take the lead,
Playing hide-and-seek with every seed.

So grab a drink, chill by the blooms,
Join the fun, ignore the glooms.
In this wild and vibrant view,
Life's a giggle, shared by few.

Sweet Tears and Sunlit Evenings

In a garden where giggles bloom,
The zinnias dance, dispelling gloom.
A bee's drunk waltz, quite absurd,
Buzzing off-key, a buzzing nerd.

Cucumbers wear their prickly coats,
While tomatoes chat like gossiping goats.
Under the sun, they sip on joy,
Sipping lemonade, oh what a ploy!

Lemon trees laugh, their fruits so bright,
Sharing their zest in sunny delight.
With every sigh, a flower sways,
Bringing on laughter in so many ways.

So let's toast to petals, and all they share,
A motley crew without a care.
In this garden, hilarity reigns,
Turning our frowns to sunshine trains.

Interludes of Green Serenity

In a patch of green, the critters play,
Chasing each other the whole day.
A frog in a tie croaks in charm,
While daisies giggle, their heads all warm.

Grasshoppers jump with silly flair,
While mushrooms preen without a care.
Snails in tuxedos, so suave and slow,
A fashion show at the base of a row.

Cacti prickle with a cheeky smile,
Making every garden trip worth the while.
They throw shade with elegance and pride,
As we laugh together, side by side.

In this haven where laughter's found,
Nature's punchlines abound, so sound.
Under the blue, let silliness brew,
In green serenades, our hearts renew.

Portals to Inner Landscapes

Open your heart, there's a door to see,
Where daisies chat with a bumblebee.
They trade sweet secrets, quite a sight,
Underneath stars that twinkle at night.

The willows whisper, telling tales,
Of socks mismatched in the wind's gales.
They giggle softly as pine trees sway,
Spinning stories in a playful ballet.

Moonlit nights, where owls wear caps,
Reading comics on old tree laps.
With every hoot, a punchline lands,
Nature's humor in subtle strands.

Portals to joy, where whimsy flows,
In laughter's embrace, the spirit grows.
Join the dance of the flora so free,
Where humor's the key to harmony.

Flora in the Portfolio of Time

Petals unfold like stories untold,
With roses knitting secrets bold.
In their laughter, the tulips peek,
Finding joy in the language of the cheeks.

Violets wearing crowns of glee,
With sunflowers saluting me.
A daisy blinks, conspiracies shared,
Planting smiles as it proudly dared.

Through seasons' change, the leaves all quip,
Nature's humor takes a joyful trip.
In the portfolio of time we see,
Flora's quirkiness, wild and free.

So let's raise a toast to our leafy friends,
On their funny tales, our laughter depends.
In this gallery where silliness thrives,
We celebrate flora, where giggle survives.

Roots of Resilience

In a pot with dinner scraps,
Lies a plant that deftly maps,
With roots that dance and twirl about,
Beneath the soil, it has no doubt.

It stretches out, a leafy grin,
With promises of life within,
A sprout of hope, a twist of fate,
As weeds complain, 'We're still too late!'

It only laughs at rainy days,
And stores its color in sun's rays,
Who knew a cactus could be wise?
It laughs back hard, with prickly sighs!

So when you feel a little drained,
Just check your pot, and be sustained,
Remember, little green delights,
Can grow with giggles, day and nights.

Savoring Moments of Radiance

Beneath the sun, the flowers grin,
Sipping dew like it's a gin,
They sway and twist, a lively dance,
Awakening those who chance.

A bumblebee with silly flair,
Bumps the blooms without a care,
While petals giggle, laugh, and sway,
Reminding us to seize the day.

A slice of cake, a heaping spoon,
Sunset's glow, we hum a tune,
Each moment cherished, colors bold,
In silly mischief, life unfolds.

So come, my friend, don't wait and pine,
Join in the dance, let's sip the shine,
We'll relish joy, snacks piled high,
In vibrant cheer, we'll touch the sky.

Embrace of the Verdant Dreamscape

In a garden filled with bright delight,
Every leaf has dreams in sight,
They whisper secrets, share a laugh,
As gnomes devise a cheeky half.

The daisies wink, a playful tease,
Swaying gently in the breeze,
With petals soft as cotton candy,
They jest about plants getting dandy.

A fern in shade begins to jest,
'I'm just too cool, much like the rest,'
While violets strut and show their flair,
They joke about the sun's hot glare.

With every sprout, there's joy anew,
In leafy laughter waltzing through,
Nature's whimsy, don't you see?
It's a play where souls roam free.

Nectar of Resilience

In jars of honey, dreams reside,
Each drop a laugh, a silly ride,
With bees in hats, and kites of gold,
Their escapades await, unfold.

They gather sweets from blooms galore,
While shouting cheers, 'Let's get some more!'
A sticky mess, an ant parade,
In sugary frolic, they've got it made.

The fruits of laughter drip and swirl,
In every twist, the flavors twirl,
A banquet laid for pals to share,
Lemon zest kisses, without a care.

So take a sip, and laugh out loud,
Join in the fun, we're all so proud,
For in each squeeze and every drop,
The nectar's joy will never stop.

A Dance Beneath the Scorched Sky

Under the sun's relentless glare,
Cacti wear party hats with flair.
They shimmy and sway, lacking a care,
With smiles that say, 'We're quite rare!'

Lizards join in with a twisty prance,
Wiggling their tails, they take a chance.
"Who knew dry lands could lead to a dance?"
"Grab a partner, it's time for romance!"

In shadows, the succulents debate,
'Is it too hot to appreciate fate?'
But water's a rumor they love to debate,
"Oh please, my friend, don't be late!"

So laugh with them under blistering rays,
This party's wild, beyond all ways.
Where prickly jokes brighten the days,
And drenching in humor, they sway and praise.

Layers of Resilience

Oh, what a sight, these layered friends,
Like cakes stacked high, they make amends.
Each slice a story that bends,
Of drought and sun, yet still transcends.

"Here's a layer of grit, it's crunchy," they cheer,
With jokes about rain they wish would appear.
"Do we brag about roots, or should we fear?
We grow through the drought, let's give a sneer!"

In a garden so patchy, they'll strut their stuff,
"Watch us glow, we're tough and rough!
Layered in laughter, it's more than enough,
No soggy business, just fanciful fluff!"

So raise your glass to this leafy delight,
To resilience that thrives in the plight.
With humor their armor, shining so bright,
They'll dance through the chaos, sheer dynamite!

Rebirth Among the Scraps

In a land where the rubbish does grow,
New sprouts emerge from the trash below.
"Out of junk, we start the show,
Who knew a can could make us glow?"

"Oh look at us, all dressed in debris!"
With laughter and quirks, they all agree.
"Messy is nifty, can't you see?
We bloom best where the wind is free!"

With tattered leaves and charred old stems,
They hold a holiday among their friends.
A festival of quirks, where humor blends,
And life's little failures lead to amends.

So raise a toast to the once forlorn,
From disaster, oh how they were reborn!
In scraps and giggles, their dreams are sworn,
To find joy in chaos, 'til a new dawn is born!

Petals Adorned in Dust

In dusty realms where petals play,
They laugh at the grime that won't go away.
"Beauty's not clean!" they call out in sway,
With colors that flaunt what others dismay.

"Covered in grit, but still a delight!"
They sparkle like stars on a moonlit night.
"Dust makes us unique, oh what a sight,
We flourish and dance, oh hold on tight!"

In pots overflowing, they chatter with glee,
"Embrace the dirt, it's like a party, you see?
Tell a joke about weeds, come share some tea,
With laughter and fun, we grow wild and free!"

So here's to the blooms with grit and with mirth,
Who teach us to laugh about life on this Earth.
Adorned in dust, they show what it's worth,
To cherish the messiness, to dance and give birth!

Fields of Enduring Light

In gardens where giggles sprout,
Laughter blooms, no doubt.
Cacti wear their sunny hats,
Cheerful in their prickly chats.

Butterflies dance, living it up,
Sipping nectar from a cup.
While daisies tell their tall tales,
Of swirling winds and happy gales.

Silly shadows play hide and seek,
Tickling petals, all unique.
Sunshine spills on every leaf,
In this joy-filled little chief.

Fields of colors, bright and bold,
A story of merriment untold.
Where every stem finds a way,
To celebrate a sunny day.

Epiphanies in Every Thorn

Oh, the wisdom in a prick,
Lifesaver or just a trick?
Nature's puzzle wrapped in greens,
Behind each thorn, laughter gleans.

Prickly friends, with tales to share,
A gentle poke, a wild scare.
They grin as you dance between,
Turns out they're not so mean!

With giggles, cracks, and silly quirks,
Every monster has its perks.
In a garden full of grins,
You'll find your luck amidst the sins.

Life's lessons write in sharp relief,
Joy blooms bright where you'd expect grief.
Embrace the thorns, let laughter win,
Who knew wisdom could be such a sin?

Whispered Secrets of Growth

Little sprouts with whispers sweet,
Sharing secrets in their fleet.
Roots entwined in playful glee,
Join the dance—oh, come and see!

Fleeting moments, buds in bloom,
Tickles in the garden loom.
As worms recite their solemn vows,
To turn the soil in raucous rows.

Mossy jokes on stones take flight,
Beneath the moon, what a sight!
Funny thoughts in every dirge,
Say it boldly—"Don't you surge!"

With dandelions laughing loud,
Among the clovers, gather 'round.
Life's a jest we've come to know,
In whispers soft, we learn to grow.

When Resilience Takes Root

Bouncing back with flair and zest,
Each tiny bud knows how to jest.
A trickster heart in the wild,
Finding joy—a playful child.

With soil hugs and rain's sweet song,
They wiggle and jiggle all day long.
When weeds pull faces, "Not today!"
Resilience rolls in a funky way.

Brambles chuckle, roots entwined,
In the face of storms, they grind.
Jokes told by the mighty flower,
Embracing every passing hour.

So dance among those leafy friends,
Where laughter blooms and never ends.
In struggles, find the humor in sight,
For even shadows crave the light.

Petals of Solitude

In a garden where silence croons,
A cactus sings to the dancing moons.
Its spines are sharp, but humor's keen,
Tickling petals, a comedic scene.

The roses gossip, the daisies laugh,
While violets plot their hilarious path.
One sunflower claims to be quite bright,
But its shade gives the joke a twist tonight.

A dandelion dreams of being a queen,
But in the winds, it's a mischievous bean.
With every puff, it spreads its cheer,
A royal seed with intent so clear.

So here's to blooms with quirky flair,
In the solitude where laughter's rare.
They thrive in jest, in sunny delight,
Petals of humor, oh what a sight!

Lavender Hues at Dusk

When dusk arrives with lavender hues,
The bees begin their baffled snooze.
Buzzing dreams of delightful pies,
While moths plan their late-night fries.

A lavender sprig, so proud in bloom,
Tells jokes that waft around the room.
The fireflies giggle, 'What's your game?'
'Just lightening up your flower name!'

In shadows deep, the humor grows,
Complaints of plants and their funny throes.
'The best part of being tall,' one sighs,
'Is watching gardeners stumble and rise!'

As twilight wraps the garden tight,
Each bloom knows laughs will take flight.
With lavender laughs and silly tunes,
They dance beneath the twinkling moons.

Beneath the Surface of Still Waters

Beneath the stillness, fish tickle the reeds,
Swap stories of worms and playful deeds.
The frogs on the lily pads wish to croak,
'I'm the king of this pond!' they'd jokingly joke.

Reflection reveals the fish in a pose,
Striking a pose that nobody knows.
The algae chuckles, 'What's the catch?'
While turtles plot a slow-motion hatch.

A swirl of laughter beneath the sheen,
Where water-dwellers find joy unseen.
The dragonflies giggle, their dance quite absurd,
Flitting like whispers, lightly unheard.

So cherish the chuckles beneath the blue,
Where every splash tells a joke or two.
In quietude lurks the fun of the pond,
Life's buoyant laughter—of it, we're fond!

Thorns, Blossoms, and Grace

Among the thorns, the blossoms flirt,
With prickly jokes that alight and hurt.
'The more you prick, the funnier we get,'
Quips a rose with a thorny mindset.

'What's the hardest part of blooming here?'
Asks a petal, poking fun with cheer.
When the sunlight hits, the thorns will shine,
In a prickly way, oh how divine!

The daisies roll with laughter and mirth,
As petals whisper, 'We know our worth.'
With thorns on the side, we bear our grace,
In the garden of humor, there's always space.

So let's embrace the beauty and jest,
In thorns and blossoms, we are blessed.
With laughter entwined in the floral trace,
There's humor in every flowered face!

From Ruins to Radiance

In a world where cacti grow,
I stumbled on a pot of dough.
It looked like mud, but oh so fine,
I laughed, 'This pizza's truly mine!'

Amidst the dust and wreckage strewn,
A dancing fern began to swoon.
It twirled around with glee and flair,
I thought, 'Who knew plants could compare?'

From shattered dreams, a bloom popped up,
Affectionately called 'Cactus Cup!'
It waved its spiky arms so bold,
I chuckled, 'This one's worth its weight in gold!'

So here's to growth from less to more,
With plants that laugh and tales galore.
In mirth we find the brightest gleam,
From ruins rise, we laugh and beam!

The Silhouettes of Strength

In shadows where the flowers dance,
A snapdragon took a chance.
With petals bold, it struck a pose,
'Hey look at me, I'm art, who knows?'

A sunflower grinned, its face so bright,
'I'll block the sun on a cloudy night!'
It stood so tall, like a superhero,
In gardens grand, it stole the show!

A tiny weed with dreams so big,
Wore a crown made from a twig.
'I'm royalty', it shouted loud,
Amongst the grass, it felt so proud!

So here's to strength in silly forms,
With plants that weather life's wild storms.
Together we find laughter's light,
In goofy shapes, we take our flight!

A Serenade for the Resilient

A hearty plant with roots so strong,
Sang a merry, mock-filled song.
'I've faced the drought, the wind, the gloom,
But still I bloom, I still consume!'

Beside it, daisies took their cue,
'Although we're short, we've moxie too!'
With tiny voices, they chimed in clear,
'Life's a dance, come join us here!'

An old bonsai told a joke,
'I've seen it all, but I won't croak!'
It cracked a smile, showing its age,
'What's life without a little stage?'

In every note of nature's tune,
Resilience blooms under the moon.
With laughter shared, we grow and sway,
In our silly serenade, we play!

The Palette of Survival

A rainbow rose with paints ablaze,
Declared with pride, 'I love these days!'
With brush in paw, it swirled delight,
'Let's splash our joy, and paint the night!'

A dandelion, with fluff so grand,
Blew wishes far with a simple hand.
'Let's make a wish, and toss it out,
Amongst the weeds, let laughter sprout!'

In pots and plots, the colors spoke,
Of stony hearts, and laughter's joke.
A riot of hues, they flounced around,
Creating joy where hope is found!

In life's grand canvas, don't you see?
All colors bloom, both you and me.
So grab your brush, let's paint it bright,
In fun and laughter, we find our light!

Beyond the Drought

In a land where cacti rock,
They hold a party in a sock.
The sun beats down, they don their shades,
It's a wild scene in green cascades.

With water guns and spritzing rains,
They dance around like carefree trains.
Every droplet's a funny cheer,
While lizards laugh, 'We'll persevere!'

The tumbleweeds join in the jest,
Trying to be their very best.
But when the storm clouds finally part,
They throw a bash, a prickly art.

So here's to pals, both tough and spry,
In desert dreams, they laugh and fly.
A twist of fate, a splash, and glee,
Beyond the drought, they're wild and free.

Whimsy of the Untamed

A mischievous cactus wearing a hat,
Twists and turns like an acrobat.
It teases the other plants in line,
Says, 'Sway like me and you'll be fine!'

The ferns and fronds, all in a whirl,
Giggling hard, doing a twirl.
They invite the bees to join the show,
With honeyed jokes, they steal the glow.

A dandelion joins with puffball grace,
Twinkle-toed in a dance and chase.
Secretly plotting a jet-fueled flight,
Should they ever dare to take to night.

So, gather round in floral delight,
Life's a giggle in the fragrant light.
In the untamed world, chaos is grand,
With laughter blooming across the land.

Shadows of Forgotten Gardens

In a garden where weeds hide the fun,
A gnome dreams of his day in the sun.
But each flower holds a shady tale,
Of daisies sneaking snacks in a pail.

The roses flirt with the morning dew,
While violets argue on who's the blue.
An artful crew, without a doubt,
They scheme to spice up the garden sprout.

The sunflowers stand tall, showing off height,
Make fun of moles who can't get it right.
Their dirt-tunneled homes make a comical sight,
Chasing bright blooms in the fall of night.

So here in shadows where laughter reigns,
Nature's surprises keep busting chains.
In forgotten corners, joy persists,
In the garden's heart, no laughter missed.

Something More Than Survival

Prickly pear plotting how to thrive,
Says, 'Let's have a feast and feel alive!'
With jagged edges and a cheeky grin,
It hosts a gathering, let the fun begin!

Succulents snug in their cozy bed,
Joking about the ants overhead.
'If they only knew our secret plan,
They'd become dessert in our grand buffet, man!'

A wise old aloe sings a tune,
'The world needs laughter, not just monsoons!'
With sprigs of thyme and rosemary cheer,
They conjure smiles, spreading heat here.

So let us celebrate this playful way,
In every moment, let laughter play.
For thriving's more than just survive,
In this green patch, we come alive!

Savoring the Sweetness Within

In a garden where giggles grow,
Laughter sprinkles seeds, just so.
Sugar-coated dreams take flight,
Bouncing on the breeze, pure delight.

Ripe berries burst with juicy cheer,
Making life's troubles disappear.
We dance like bees from bloom to bloom,
Chasing the sweetness, never gloom.

Butterflies gossip in the warm sun,
They whisper secrets, 'Aren't we fun?'
With wings of charm, they twirl around,
In this rich garden, joy is found.

So let's munch on moments, never dread,
Savoring each gulp, not just the bread.
Giggles pop like fizzy drinks,
Here's to the sweetness, what do you think?

Oasis of the Soft Spirit

In a desert where cactus dance,
We sip coconut with a flirty glance.
Palm trees sway, oh, what a sight,
Making the sand feel just right.

Sunbeams tickle soft shades of green,
Creating a scene that's pure and serene.
With each wave of laughter, we dive deep,
Into pools of joy, no need to weep.

Sipping drinks with umbrellas on top,
The giggles bubble, they never stop.
We float on laughter, a buoyant ride,
In this oasis of mirth, we abide.

So join the fun in the warm embrace,
Where softness tickles and smiles race.
Life's a beach party, come take a seat,
An oasis of joy, oh, what a treat!

Sips of Solace in Stillness

In the quiet where giggles hide,
We sip sweet tea with a knowing pride.
Lemon zest and honey swirl,
Tickling tongues in a joyful whirl.

Calm moments, but oh so loud,
With laughter echoing from the crowd.
The stillness hums a silly tune,
As we sip in the lazy afternoon.

Cookies crumble, laughter spills,
In every sip, we chase those thrills.
Sweet sips of solace, a fumble or two,
Life's little messes make it all new.

So raise your cup, toast to the fun,
In the calm, where we all run.
Let's laugh softly, then burst out loud,
For sweet moments, we're always proud!

Tangled Roots of Kindred Spirits

In a grove where giggles intertwine,
We share stories, foolish yet fine.
Roots tangled deeply in the ground,
With each other, joy is found.

Whimsical branches sway with grace,
As we frolic in this lively space.
Laughter bubbles like a brook,
As kindred spirits read the good book.

Tangled up like a playful vine,
We celebrate our quirks, so divine.
With every chuckle, we grow tall,
Embracing oddities, we stand enthralled.

So let's plant seeds of laughter bright,
In this forest of friendship, pure delight.
Together we flourish, roots and all,
In twisted tales, we hear the call!

Harvest of Hidden Wonders

In the garden of my dreams, I tread,
Where laughter blooms and worries shed.
I trip over giggles, oh what a sight,
Grapes of joy roll into the night.

With carrots wearing funny hats,
And broccoli dancing with the chats.
Tomatoes blush, they're quite the tease,
As munching bunnies do as they please.

Cucumbers whisper secrets low,
While pumpkins boast of their grand show.
Each fruit a tale, each veggie a jest,
In this harvest, we're truly blessed.

So gather round, let's feast and cheer,
For hidden wonders bring us near.
With every bite, a giggle's found,
In this jolly garden, joy abounds.

Thirsting for Connection

In a world of sips and slurps so wide,
I search for friends on this wild ride.
With lemonade laughs and soda streams,
Our bubbles burst into silly dreams.

The cactus asks why I'm so shy,
As I guzzle water, oh my, oh my!
A watermelon waves from a sunny spot,
Says, "Join the party, give it a shot!"

Straws intertwine like our silly fate,
And each sweet sip makes us celebrate.
With every chug, our worries flee,
A toast to friendship, just you and me.

So let us quench this thirsty plight,
With laughter flowing, spirits in flight.
In the jugs of joy, we will find,
The sweetest connection, intertwined.

Oasis of Forgotten Hopes

In the desert of my mind, I roam,
Hopes like cacti, finding a home.
A tumbleweed rolls with a wink,
Sipping sunshine, we share a drink.

The mirage giggles, making me sway,
"Come play in the sand," it seems to say.
With whispers of dreams that once wore a crown,
We laugh at the shadows that tried to drown.

Lizards with shades take quite the break,
As we build castles from some dust flake.
Each grain a memory, each smile a sun,
In this odd oasis, we frolic and run.

So join the parade of forgotten cheer,
For hopes sprout laughter, that's crystal clear.
In this quirky land where wishes bloom,
Let's dance in the light with joy in the room.

Radiance of Unseen Beauty

In the art of quirks, there's beauty to find,
With rainbow chickens that strut and unwind.
A sparrow in sunglasses, quite the delight,
Sings a tune that takes flight in the night.

Under stars that giggle, the moon winks wide,
While shadows of laughter play on the side.
There's charm in the clumsy, grace in the fall,
With each little slip, we have a ball.

Forget all the glitz and the polished sheen,
For charm lies in wisdom that's yet to be seen.
With mismatched socks and hearts that collide,
We bask in the glow where true smiles abide.

So raise up your hands to the odd and bizarre,
For beauty lives boldly, like a shooting star.
In this world of laughter and quirky decree,
Radiance awaits, just you and me.

The Art of Growing Softly

In a pot of plenty, I take my stand,
With leaves like fingers, I wave my hand.
Water me gently, but not too much,
I prefer a sip, not a full-on crutch.

Sunshine, oh sunshine, my favorite friend,
But don't bake me crisp, or my fun will end.
I like to lounge, all fleshy and bright,
If I could wear shades, oh what a sight!

Friends all around me, a quirky crew,
Some spiky, some fuzzy, and all of us blue.
We laugh at the weeds, so jealous and green,
While sipping our dew, feeling quite serene.

So here's to the soft ones, with humor and cheer,
We thrive on the laughter, that's why we're all here.
Growing together in our snug little space,
In the art of growing, we've found our grace.

Tapestry of Vibrant Reflections

In pots of laughter, we sprout and sway,
With colors that brighten the dullest of day.
Mirrors of sunshine, we bask and we glow,
The perfect reflection of life's little show.

Some wear their spines like a crown on their head,
While others just giggle, avoiding all dread.
With roots intertwined, a goofy parade,
Creating a quilt that will never fade.

Oh, how we chatter through storms and through sun,
Making new jokes, playing just for fun.
Each droplet of water, a splash of delight,
We're vibrant reflections, a colorful sight!

So gather around, for a gardener's treat,
We'll share all our secrets with roots at our feet.
In this tapestry woven of laughter and spice,
We'll bask in the joy, oh, isn't it nice?

Echoes of the Nurturing Void

In the quietest corner, we huddle and thrive,
In the nurturing void, we feel so alive.
We sip on the whispers, the secrets of earth,
With each little giggle, we celebrate birth.

Silly little critters come visit our space,
With wiggly bodies and smiles on their face.
They dance on our leaves, with no care at all,
While we offer them shade, in our leafy hall.

Our shadows sway gently, a calming ballet,
In the heart of the void, we frolic and play.
Beneath the full moon, our laughter takes flight,
We feast on the silence that blankets the night.

So here's to the echoes, the giggles we find,
In the nurturing void, we leave woes behind.
With roots deep in laughter, we flourish and grow,
In the warmth of connection, we all steal the show.

Succor of the Sun-Kissed Bloom

With petals of joy, I reach for the sky,
In a sun-kissed daze, I twirl and I sigh.
A nudge from the sunlight, my dance comes alive,
Who knew being soft could make me so thrive?

Fellow blooms giggle as we stretch our stems,
While insects join in, singing silly gems.
We sway in the breeze, like a quirky crew,
In this garden of laughter, where worries are few.

A sprinkle of humor, a dash of delight,
We come together, all jolly and bright.
With bees as our DJs, buzzing the tunes,
We'll dance with abandon, beneath the big moons.

So here's to the softies, the gigglers and glow,
We celebrate life with a colorful show.
With blossoms that chuckle, and roots packed with cheer,

In the sun-kissed blooms, we'll always be near.

Threads of Unyielding Grace

In a garden so bright, with greens on display,
Plants wear their smiles, in a quirky array.
Each leaf a little dancer, twirling around,
Waving at insects, in laughter they're found.

Roots stretch and giggle, deep down in the ground,
"Hey, look at me!" they whisper, no need to be proud.
Sharing their secrets with worms that pass through,
While daisies gossip, as flowers often do.

Sunshine gives golden hugs to the day,
While raindrops play tag, in a playful ballet.
With every new sprout, a tale to be spun,
Nature's own humor, delightfully fun!

So, let's raise a glass to each whimsical sprout,
Their silly adventures, they never doubt.
For in this green world, where laughter must grow,
The threads of delight weave a tapestry glow!

Portraits of the Unseen

Behind every leaf, a portrait is drawn,
Of sleepy old bugs that linger at dawn.
A worm with a mustache, so proud and so fine,
Claims a seed as his throne, with flair and design.

The butterfly winks from her perch on a rose,
While snails shell-shuffle, in elegant clothes.
Each creature, a character, full of surprise,
In this leafy gallery, where laughter would rise.

Squirrels paint mischief with acorn confetti,
While frogs hold a concert, all jumpy and sweaty.
"Leap higher!" they croak while the world spins around,
In this theater of nature, joy knows no bounds.

So come take a peek at the unseen delight,
In gardens and corners, where laughter takes flight.
Each little inhabitant dons a new role,
Creating a masterpiece, a whimsical scroll!

Nature's Quiet Rebellion

The cactus wears spikes, in a punk fashion flair,
While daisies conspire to overthrow air!
"Why should we sit in this neat little line?
Let's dance in the wind, over here we'll entwine!"

The mountains shake hands with the clouds in a fuss,
"It's fluffy up here, let's make a big fuss!"
And rivers revolt, with a splash and a whirl,
While frogs call the shots in their swampy swirl.

Petunias rebel, with colors so wild,
"Be bold!" they chant, "Let's not be beguiled!"
In the quietest corners, life brews a plot,
In this garden of whimsy, there's mischief a lot.

With laughter around us, in nature's domain,
We join in the fun, not a moment of pain.
For each tiny riot is a reason to sing,
In a world that's so silly, let's dance and take wing!

Dreaming Lush in the Silence

In the hush of the night, when the world's feeling bold,
Leaves share their dreams, as their stories unfold.
"Did you see that star? It spun like a top!
And what of that comet? It went with a plop!"

A bed of soft moss whispers secrets so sweet,
"Let's build a sandcastle for critters to meet!"
With a wink from a firefly, all glowy and bright,
The creatures unite for a whimsical night.

In the shadows, a gopher spins tales of the lore,
Of wormy adventures in tunnels galore.
They chuckle together, with all of their might,
As the moon beams down and joins in the flight.

So dream lush and full in the silence so grand,
Where every soft chuckle is a soft, gentle hand.
For in quiet places, where laughter takes hold,
The spirit of mischief adds magic untold!

Echoes of Hushed Resilience

In the cracks of a sidewalk, they poke their heads,
Rebellious little green things, breaking new beds.
With a wink and a nod, they sprout and tease,
"Who needs a garden? We thrive with such ease!"

When rain starts to laugh like a tickling friend,
These tiny warriors just start to ascend.
They wiggle and jiggle, no need for a plan,
In a world full of concrete, they're Nature's big fans.

Whispers of triumph in each little leaf,
Ignoring all droughts, they're the kings of belief.
They throw a great party, all vibrant and spry,
Dance with the sunlight, wave roots to the sky!

With every new sprout, they're a jolly brigade,
Making fun of the sun, saying, "We're not afraid!"
Each layer of dough might be flat as a stone,
But they'll rise like the bread that's just found its own tone.

A Garden Born from Stone

In crevices cozy, the mischief unfolds,
Cranky old rocks now wear plant bits like gold.
With laughter and glee, they tickle the crust,
"We're not just survivors, we're rooted in trust!"

Amongst stubborn gravel, they plot a small coup,
Each cactus a spy, plotting what's new.
In lip-smacking sun, they bask and they grin,
"You think we need soil? Come join the spin!"

A flower pops up, with a cheeky red hue,
"What's dirt, anyway? I don't need a view!"
Stones shake in fright, just a crusty old crew,
Yet here come our greens, waving proudly anew.

They giggle at winters and whisper at rains,
Dodging the freeze with their silly refrains.
A garden in stone? Oh, what a delight!
These jokers are bold, keeping spirits so bright.

Verdant Dreams in Parched Soil

In a desert of dreams, they bounce like a ball,
Sipping on sunbeams, they answer the call.
While others are snoozing, they break out in dance,
"Who needs all that water? We're taking a chance!"

Dunes rolling 'round, with a grin on their face,
These greens are quite spry, in a race for their place.
With roots that hold tight, they defy every season,
"We're not feeling thirsty, that's just our decision!"

With laughter like sand, they shimmer and sway,
Playing hide and seek with the clouds on their way.
A party of colors, a carnival spree,
"Parched soil? What's that? We live wild and free!"

From ashes and dust, they emerge with a flair,
Pleased as a punch, they toss up some cheer.
In a banquet of light and a feast of the bold,
Flourishing brightly, like stories retold.

The Language of Resilience

In the chatter of leaves, they flit and they flutter,
Communicating secrets, giddy with utter.
"Root for each other! That's what we do!"
Living our lives in each shade and each hue."

They've got their own lingo, with gestures so spry,
A wink of a petal or a seed tossed on high.
While the world talks of clouds and shadowy worries,
They giggle and jive, racing through pearly flurries.

In the symphony sung by the trees and the breeze,
They're the maestros hitting all the right keys.
"Who cares if it rains? We'll dance by the brook!
Life's a great novel, just take a good look!"

So here's to the ones with their laughter so bold,
Who take all the hardships and turn them to gold.
In the grand choir of nature, they jest and they play,
Resilience is chuckling in the sun's old ballet!

Veins of Life and Light

In the garden of oddities, we grow,
With plants that talk and plants that glow.
They whisper secrets, they tell a joke,
Even the weeds wear a funny cloak.

Sunshine tickles the leaves so green,
As the fruits wear hats, like kings, they're seen.
A tomato danced, a cucumber sighed,
In this wild world, joy can't hide.

The carrots wear shades, what a sight!
Dancing around under the bright moonlight.
A potato juggles, not quite on cue,
While the peas cheer in a lively hue.

So come join the fun in this strange space,
Nature's circus brings smiles to your face.
With laughter in the air, we'll play our part,
In the veins of life, where mischief starts.

Fables of the Forgotten Earth

Once a cabbage dreamed of the sea,
Wishing of waves and wild jubilee.
It packed its leaves, set sail in style,
On a boat made of lettuce, oh what a mile!

The radish recited a poetic line,
While carrots debated the best way to dine.
A parsnip wore glasses to look quite wise,
In the tales of dirt, there's always a surprise.

A dandelion flaunted a crown of gold,
Declaring its reign, brave and bold.
While the mushrooms chuckled, hiding away,
In the shadows of stories, they love to play.

As the earth spins tales that always amuse,
With roots that connect like vibrant hues.
In this garden where laughter holds sway,
Nature pens fables in its own quirky way.

Quintessence of the Daring Heart

In the wilds of bravery, we dare to thrive,
This heart beats strong, oh, how it strives!
With glittery courage, we dance and shout,
Shielded in laughter, casting doubt out.

A brave little fig, with a crown so fine,
Fancies itself the king of the vine.
Telling tall tales to all who dare,
As squirrels gather, gasping for air.

A bold cactus pricks misconceptions around,
Claiming that comfort can also be found.
Jumping with glee, it leads the way,
In the mosaic of life, we laugh and sway.

So raise up your glass filled with fruity cheer,
To the daring hearts that make the world clear.
In the garden of dreams, take your sweet part,
For joy is the essence of the daring heart.

Nectar of Endurance

In the hive of the buzzing, sweet delight,
Bees make jokes that take flight.
They swirl and twirl in nectar's embrace,
Each drop holds laughter, a sweetened face.

A flower shivers in the breezy glow,
Tickling the bees down below.
As they chant, "Buzz on, don't be shy,"
In this dance of endurance, we all fly high.

The roses giggle in the soft sunlight,
Petals blushing with all their might.
While the daisies chuckle in a carefree way,
Reminding us laughter is here to stay.

So sip from the cup of this wondrous cheer,
In the nectar of joy, hold your dear.
For through the struggles, hum and sing,
Endurance is sweet—let your heart take wing.

A Tapestry of Thorns

In the garden of woes, I often tread,
With prickly friends, they're like a spread.
Smiling at pain, what a bizarre flair,
Who knew thorns could offer such a snare?

Bumbling bumblebees with their buzz so loud,
Mumble about life as if they're proud.
Cactus claims it's the best in the game,
But every sharp jab feels like shame!

We toast to our wounds with spicy hot sauce,
While giggling at nature's rude little boss.
Each poke a reminder of laughs we share,
In the prickly embrace of life laid bare.

So here's to the thorns, and cheers to the mess,
In this tapestry woven, we count our excess.
Let's dance with the jabs, in joy we delight,
For a hearty laugh makes our worries take flight.

Oasis of the Forgotten

In a land where water laughs at the sun,
Lies an oasis where no one will run.
Forgotten by fortune, or maybe by fate,
It bubbles with dreams, but they're always late.

Palm trees flap arms like they're waving hello,
While sand dunes gossip beneath the moon's glow.
Old camels munching on wisdom so stale,
Whispering secrets of some bygone tale.

Mirages are pranks, just a heatwave's jest,
Turning the traveler into a mere quest.
In a glass of half-empty, we clink our cups,
Who knew deserts had so many hiccups?

The forgotten blend in like they belong,
Sipping on mirth with a side of a song.
Let's toast to the heat and the laughs that we share,
For joy blooms like laughter, if you really don't care.

Grace in Drought

When rain plays hard to get, oh what a sight,
Cacti post selfies, feeling so bright.
"Look at my curves!" the succulents delight,
As they bask in the struggle, holding on tight.

I water my worries with hopes and some dreams,
Yet watch them evaporate, bursting at seams.
Dancing in dust with an elegant air,
Laughing at droughts, cause we just don't care!

The lizards play limbo, swinging so low,
While tumbleweeds tumble in comedy show.
"Grace in drought's not a trick, just pure charm,"
They say as they frolic, arms wide and warm.

So here's to the barren that tickle us still,
In the drought's dry embrace, life's comedic thrill.
With laughter as nectar, let's raise a toast,
For every dry moment, we cherish the most.

The Essence of Survival

Survival's an art, full of quirks and quirks,
Like blending in weeds and pretending it works.
Nature's own jesters, we dance and we sway,
'Cause life's but a play, in a quirky ballet!

With roots made of rubber, we stretch and we bend,
Become masters of shade, on ourselves we depend.
Through drought and through flood, we're packed with glee,
Our laughter is nectar, our anthem, "Just be!"

Every wilted petal is merely a prank,
A trick of the light, we've climbed from the tank.
Mimicking laughter in tight little lines,
Life's essence is wrapped in kaleidoscope signs.

So, here's to the dance of the twisted vines,
To surviving the jest with our own punchy rhymes.
When faced with defeat, we'll skip and we'll twirl,
For the essence of survival is priceless, my girl!

Whispers of Calm Desires

In the garden of whimsy, I found a delight,
A pickle jar giggling, in the soft moonlight.
Chasing dreams like fireflies, spinning around,
With laughter so sweet, like candy unbound.

The daisies conspire with mischievous glee,
Telling secrets in colors, just for me.
With a wink and a nod, they twist and they dance,
In a wild waltz of joy, oh, what a chance!

Yet, who knew that weeds had such clever appeal?
A party of thorns, a soft-hearted deal.
They dressed up in laughter, hid under a hat,
"Caution!" they giggled, "Watch out for the cat!"

So I tiptoed around, with a chuckle and grin,
Joined the flower party, let the fun begin.
In the whispering breeze, a soft promise spun,
"Life's a jest, dear friend, let's have some fun!"

Blooming in Shadows

In corners unseen where the shadows peek,
A cactus is sketching, quite daring and sleek.
It paints with its prickles, a whimsical sight,
I swear it can tickle with laughter at night.

The moon in her wisdom, teases the blooms,
Their giggles bounce softly in magical rooms.
As the sun stretches out, with a yawn and a sigh,
The flowers all whisper, "Oh me, oh my!"

A secret soirée, with colors so bright,
Dandelions shaking under stars of the night.
They toast with their petals, sweet nectar divine,
While grasshoppers croon in a rhythm so fine.

The shadows are lively, no need for disguise,
With a snicker and punchline, they open their eyes.
So here in this glee, where the daylight won't set,
We're blooming together, without any fret!

Lush Dreams in Arid Lands

In a desert so dry, where the sun reigns supreme,
There's a mirage of laughter, a whimsical dream.
A tumbleweed tumbles, with zest in its spin,
Singing songs of cactus, with a cheeky grin.

"Why do we worry about rain coming down?
We're just a bunch of jokers, let's wear a crown!"
The sands start to giggle, a soft, sandy laugh,
As lizards flip scripts, in this hilarious path.

With cacti for friends, and shadows for shade,
We throw a big party, no plans to evade.
In the rays of the sun, our antics unfold,
Each prickly embrace, a treasure to hold.

When the moonlight arrives, we'll twirl in delight,
In lush, sandy dreams, we'll bloom through the night.
With no tanks holding water, and no gardener's hand,
Our laughter's enough, in these arid lands!

Heart of a Cactus

There's a heart in the cactus, all prickly and warm,
In a world full of giggles, it sure knows the charm.
With a bounce and a wiggle, it greets every soul,
Embracing the jesters, it's the life of the goal.

"Come one, come all, let's dance in the sun,
With a jolt of green giggles, oh isn't it fun?"
It jabs with affection, then melts into cheer,
Even cacti believe that life's meant to hear!

When the stars finally peek from the blanket of night,
The cactus hums softly, its colors ignite.
With twinkling delight, it shakes out its spines,
Turning prickers to softies, as happiness shines.

Each creature around, joins in for a laugh,
Swapping tales of mischief, no more from the past.
For deep in the desert, where wisdom is spun,
The heart of a cactus beats softly in fun!

Lush Lullabies of the Heart

In a garden where giggles grow,
Silly shadows dance to and fro.
Petals make snickers, leaves share a tease,
Nature's jokes bring you to your knees.

Worms wear hats, it's quite absurd,
While bees recite lines, each one a word.
Fruits crack jokes, so juicy and bright,
Who knew veggies could ignite such delight?

Sunbeams tickle the blooms with glee,
A cool breeze whispers, 'Just be free!'
Laughter bubbles like sap from trees,
In this wacky world, just take it with ease.

So come, dear friend, share in the fun,
Join the circus of blossoms, let's run!
In this lush realm where giggles abound,
Joy is the harvest, and love's all around.

Elixirs of Endurance

Cacti wear shades, sipping sun all day,
While succulents giggle in their own way.
Smoothies of laughter, they blend with cheer,
Gulp down the joy, and don't shed a tear.

In a pot of whimsy, herbs burst with jokes,
Chili peppers crack up, sharing their pokes.
Thyme makes puns, while mint is a tease,
Even basil laughs with the greatest of ease.

Stories bubble like tea on the stove,
Resilience brewed in every grove.
Green thumbs high-five with plans so absurd,
Competing for who tells the best word.

So let's raise a toast to the plants that thrive,
Who giggle and wiggle and feel so alive!
In this garden of humor, let's spread the cheer,
Making memories that last through the year.

Cradle of Verdant Whispers

In a meadow where laughter sows,
Whispers of greens hum sweet prose.
Leaves rustle secrets, petals play coy,
Foliage frolics, oh what a joy!

Bouncing blooms display their charm,
Wiggly worms don't mean any harm.
Succulent smiles grow wide and bright,
They tickle the air, sheer delight!

Clouds giggle softly, sketching the skies,
While roots tell stories that never lie.
Sprouts chuckle and beam in the light,
Celebrating the silly, day and night.

Come dance with the daisies, let's sway and spin,
Join the laughter where joy can begin.
In this cradle of whispers and mirth so dear,
We'll nurture our souls, year after year.

Serene Canyons of Emotion

In valleys where chuckles echo and roll,
Breeze carries tales that feed the soul.
Laughter leaps through canyon doors,
Nature's symphony forever roars.

Pebbles join in with a tap-tap tune,
Lizards make faces beneath the moon.
Sprightly shadows waltz on the stone,
Each crevice and curve feels like home.

Whimsical winds sweep up the dust,
Filling the air with giggles we trust.
Feelings sprout like wildflower seeds,
Watered with humor, growing our needs.

So trek through these canyons, joyfully roam,
Gathering laughter, it's all that we own.
With hearty smiles, let's raise our voices,
In these serene spaces, embrace our choices.

Solace in the Unyielding

In the garden's quirkiest part,
A cactus wore a vibrant hat.
He claimed it brought him lots of cheer,
But all it did was make him fat.

The ferns joked, swayed with delight,
"You'll never roll, you're stuck in sight!"
Yet he chuckled, bloated and bold,
"I'm living life, just watch me hold!"

A broccoli tried to dance one day,
But tripped on roots, oh what a play!
Lettuce laughed, gave him a shove,
"In this patch, I'm the one you love!"

So here in this patch of odd and glee,
Every leaf, a friend to see.
Together roots, tangled and tense,
Find joy in nature's, jester's nonsense.

A Song for the Unseen Blossoms

In shadows where the wild things grow,
A whisper sings to those below.
Petals peek, their colors bright,
"Oh hide and seek, what a lovely night!"

A dandelion wished for some fame,
"I won't be just a weed with shame!"
She puffed out seeds in a grand blow,
And laughed at the winds -"I steal the show!"

Violets hid in sweet retreat,
Wishing for sunlight, oh so sweet.
But a funny bee buzzed by to say,
"You're all the rage, come dance and play!"

And so they sway, a playful crew,
Dancing under skies so blue.
In this garden, loud and bright,
Life's a jest, a cheerful sight.

Heartbeats of Fresh Beginnings

On a sprouty stage, the bulbs take cheer,
Reminding all that spring is near.
With roots that wiggle and leaves that jiggle,
One broke out in a silly giggle.

Carrots dressed in neon flair,
Flashed their greens without a care.
"Don't hide below, come shine with me!"
Tomatoes yelled, "You're all so free!"

Radishes chuckled under the ground,
Whispering secrets, loud and profound.
"We thrive in dirt, that's our decree!"
"Fresh starts happen under each tree!"

With nature's laughter in the air,
Every sprout beyond compare.
Flip-flop roots in turf so true,
Finding joy in all they do.

Timeless Petals of Strength

There's strength in colors bright and bold,
Whispering tales of old retold.
A sunflower strutted with great flair,
"Each petal's armor is bold declare!"

In every wind, a proud refrain,
"To stand so tall is to endure pain!"
With snappy responses, they'd tease the sun,
"Oh golden glare, can you handle fun?"

Zinnias wild danced on parade,
Flashing their shapes, unafraid.
"Watch us swirl in vibrant hues!"
"We'll dazzle you, we're never blue!"

Timeless petals sway and grin,
Finding the light that shines within.
In this garden, strength is found,
With laughter echoing all around.

www.ingramcontent.com/pod-product-compliance
Lightning Source LLC
Chambersburg PA
CBHW070313120526
44590CB00017B/2652